The Bullfrog & The Butterfly
© Copyright 2021 Kevin Ray Decker
Published by Glorybound Publishing, Camp Verde, AZ
SAN 256-4564
Published in the United States of America
KDP ISBN 9798534573282
Copyright data is available on file.
Decker, Kevin Ray, 1962-
      The Bullfrog & The Butterfly/Kevin Ray Decker
1. Children's Books   3.Title
www.gloryboundpublishing.com

The Bullfrog & The Butterfly

by Kevin Ray Decker

Published by
Glorybound Publishing 2021

Glorybound Publishing
Camp Verde, Arizona

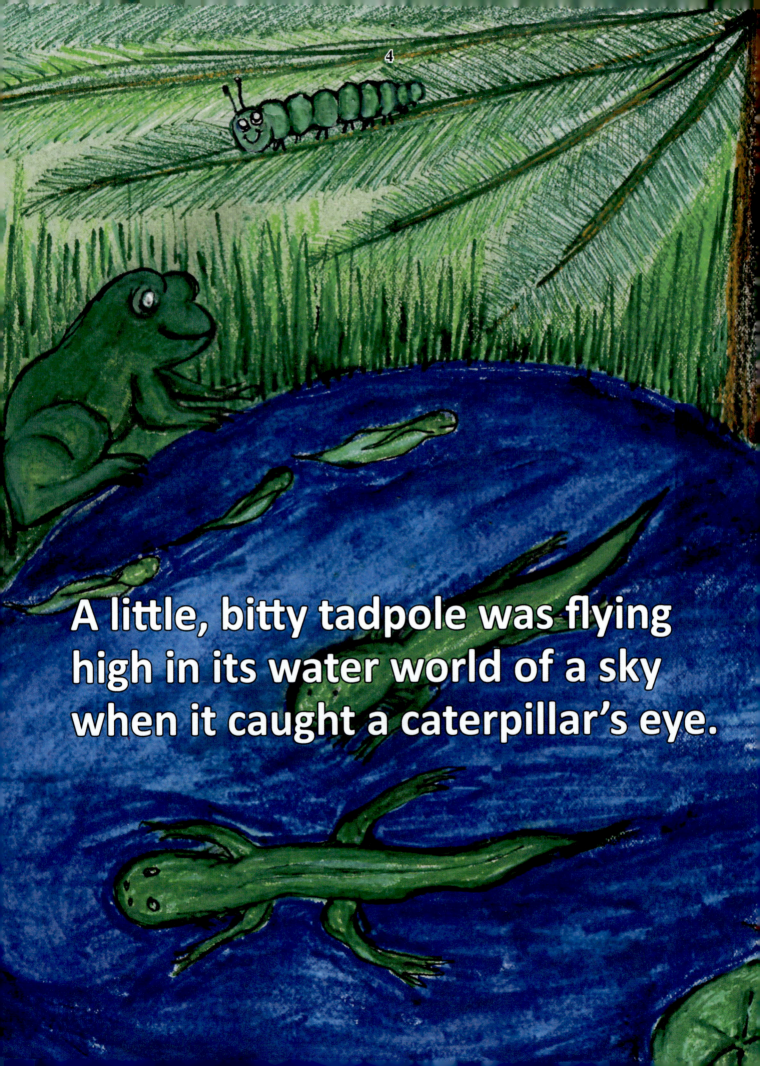

A little, bitty tadpole was flying high in its water world of a sky when it caught a caterpillar's eye.

and by instinct and luck and keeping the shiny side up,

So, there must be more to metamorphosis than meets the eye.

His gills will disappear and he soon will breathe air. He will join all the other creatures on dry land where caterpillars and butterflies and bullfrogs are on the menu, too.

All summer long Jeremiah would sing his mating song and when wintertime came it was time to hibernate again. Mr. Bullfrog was left to dig a hole and escape from winter's icy grip

They would all be headed south where Winter's through and springtime begins to make all things new.

When summer is over and winter begins Katmandeaux and all of his friends will be returning home again where its warm and sunshiny

by riding the strong winds that the spring storms bring

they come around each year bringing joy and cheer and flowerful meetings of pollen and plants, while doing the dance of romance all summer long

to Jeremiah the Bullfrog's song of "Joy to the World."

In The Family Tree.

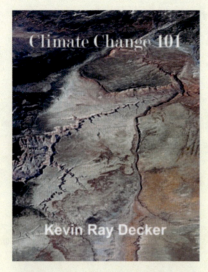
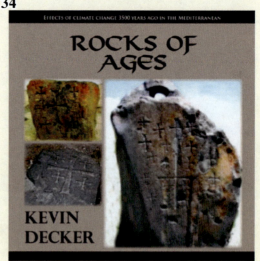
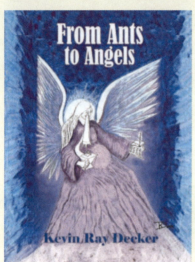
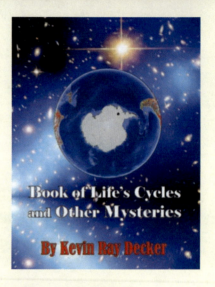

TO: NOAH
Kevin R. Decker

To contact the author:
katfishkevin@gmail.com.
Amazon.com
Phone at 928-567-3340

Made in the USA
Middletown, DE
14 September 2021